Balers

Connor Dayton

PowerKiDS press™

New York

Published in 2012 by The Rosen Publishing Group, Inc.
29 East 21st Street, New York, NY 10010

First Edition

Editor: Jennifer Way
Book Design: Greg Tucker

Photo Credits: Cover, p. 5 © www.iStockphoto.com/Cameron Pashak; p. 7 © www.iStockphoto.com/ Chris Hellyar; pp. 9, 24 (top right) © Fancy/Veer/age fotostock; pp. 10–11, 13, 14–15, 21, 22–23, 24 (top left, bottom) Shutterstock.com; p. 17 © www.iStockphoto.com/esemelwe; pp. 18–19 © www.iStockphoto.com/Marek Uliasz.

Library of Congress Cataloging-in-Publication Data

Dayton, Connor.
 Balers / by Connor Dayton. — 1st ed.
    p. cm. — (Farm machines)
 Includes index.
 ISBN 978-1-4488-4949-9 (library binding) — ISBN 978-1-4488-5048-8 (pbk.) — ISBN 978-1-4488-5049-5 (6-pack)
 1. Haying equipment—Juvenile literature. I. Title.
 TJ1485.D387 2012
 633.2'086—dc22

                                        2010049480

Manufactured in the United States of America

CPSIA Compliance Information: Batch #WS11PK: For Further Information contact Rosen Publishing, New York, New York at 1-800-237-9932

Contents

Balers wrap hay into **bales**. The first balers were called hay presses.

Tractors pull balers.

Different balers make different-shaped bales. Some make **rectangular** bales.

Some balers make round bales. Round bales are the most common.

There are teeth at the front of the baler. They pick up the hay.

The hay is
shaped inside
the baler.

Next the bale is wrapped. Then the bale drops out of the baler.

Bales are held together with twine. Twine is a strong string.

Hay feeds a farm's animals.
Horses eat mostly hay.

Balers are important farm machines!